Finders Keepers

Thematic Unconventional Poems

Curated by Diiva Dhanoya and Tarun Agarwal

Poets' Choice®
Poets Choice®

Published By

Poets Choice

Poets Choice

Poets Choice and Free Spirit LLC

1216 Broadway Floor 2 PMB 1010 - New York NY 10001 - USA

www.poetschoice.in

Phone: +1 914-650-2747 (Primary) +1 646 974 9406 (Fax)

1st Edition June 2025

Book Design by Laura Antonioli, United Kingdom
Cover Design by Koni Deraz, Germany
Editing by Kaneez Zehra Razavi, India
Curated by Diiva Dhanoya and Tarun Agarwal

Printed In India

ISBN: 978-93-6617-768-7

BCID: 690-17588380
Use it here - www.bookcrossing.com

Price: $30

About this book:

Instagram - @poetschoice

Youtube - @PoetsChoice

Poems in this book are from:
Belgium, Canada, France, Hong Kong, Kenya, India, Ireland, Northern Mariana Islands & United States

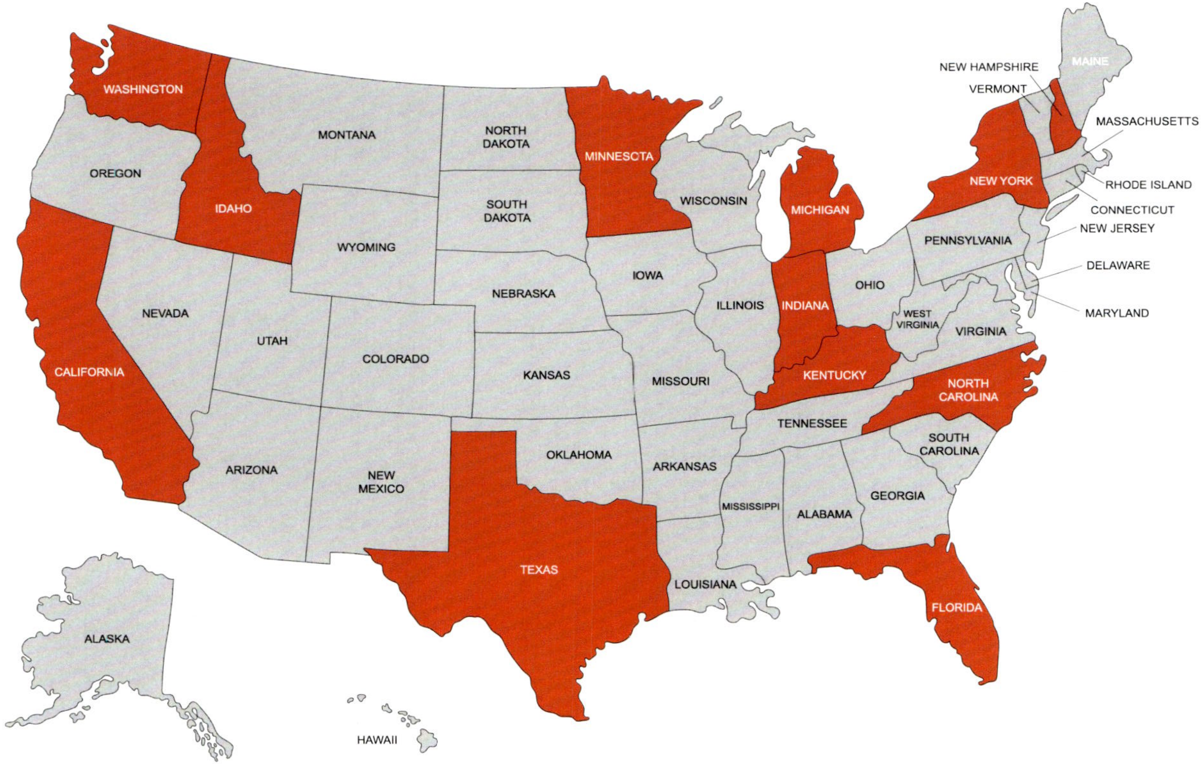
MAINE
NEW HAMPSHIRE
VERMONT
MASSACHUSETTS
RHODE ISLAND
CONNECTICUT
NEW JERSEY
DELAWARE
MARYLAND
WASHINGTON
MONTANA
NORTH DAKOTA
MINNESCTA
OREGON
IDAHO
SOUTH DAKOTA
WISCONSIN
MICHIGAN
NEW YORK
WYOMING
PENNSYLVANIA
IOWA
NEBRASKA
NEVADA
ILLINOIS
INDIANA
OHIO
UTAH
WEST VIRGINIA
VIRGINIA
COLORADO
CALIFORNIA
KANSAS
MISSOURI
KENTUCKY
NORTH CAROLINA
TENNESSEE
SOUTH CAROLINA
OKLAHOMA
ARIZONA
ARKANSAS
NEW MEXICO
MISSISSIPPI
ALABAMA
GEORGIA
TEXAS
LOUISIANA
FLORIDA
ALASKA
HAWAII

Table of Contents

Burning Questions

Annie Kuster

Washington, District of Columbia - United States

My father feared for my life and so he saved it. It only took four phone calls, and for that I am ashamed. Homes and hearts are made of glass, and mine was none the different.

Can I make a call on the way?

My father feared for my apartment and so he took me from it. Boxes from babyhood and impressions of my mother's daughter; *you're back,* he announced though I hadn't existed in this bedroom in a decade. The mobs can't find us here. The mobs can find us anywhere; hose in rainwater or foam in sea; the way your glasses fog when your mask is fastened but if you perch it *just so,* it's tolerable.

Have you ever thought—?
Really?

My mother's fallen in love with me twice and yet we're going through it. She holds my silhouette in the gold of her irises; when her eyelashes grow wet, I feel the weight of it. We speak and say nothing. Sit, say everything. She is sorry (I am sure of it). Words catch on the moisture between her lips and tongue, but every move she makes towards me echoes. She is sorry, but not for her. For the actions of others. For the actions of "them," who incite pain.

Not even for a moment?

My mother calls her mother "pain". She says it's in the ass, but I know she feels it all over. Her heart hurts when she thinks too hard about my grandmother; like Rapunzel, Grandmom is trapped in a tower without a door. Only now there is a vaccine. Only now there are coups.

Abuelita, *would you let down your hair*
or por lo menos *your guard?*

My grandmother gifts me gold-plated earrings for when I get married. She loves the idea of me in white, walking towards a man who is a stranger. She tells me her gold-filigree china will look nice in my marriage bed. I tell her my marriage bed may be in China. She laughs like she understands the depth of my desire to flee, but she has lived here for 44 years. We walk around with post-it notes, preparing for what will never happen. Her shadow breathes beneath the neon marked by my name. I want nothing more than the reflection of her Spanish eyes in my own, but I claim her spoon collection. The photos of my great-grandparents. Her paintings. Finders, keepers, I might say. Behind each wooden door appear more gold filigree and more necronym promises. Another sweater. Some teacups. An earring.

It doesn't have to be you. For you, I mean, could it be— ?

My grandfather was reincarnated as a blue jay.

So you do want it?

My great-great-grandmother was a female general, we think, though the stories often change. My father tells me I am fearless like her, though I have forgotten what that feels like. Terrified, I build homes between the bones of my chest when I cannot face what's outside me. The mob cannot find me here. The mob can find me anywhere—look at my irises, golden like my mother's. Painful. Filled to the brim with unsaid apologies.

What can I do then, for you?

My home is on fire and I am the arsonist. I left a stove on when making that recipe I'm trying. To be a better cook. More. Complete. A love letter I lit with a match; a murder of my most egregious memories. A curling iron from the time I tried to look pretty, for you. Flammable, like fear. Like pitchforks. You can't light gold-filigree china on fire, but marriages burn without gasoline. So does democracy, and towers.

Can't come with me, where I'm going

Cold Shoulder

Vasilisa Marinchenko

Dublin, Ontario - Ireland

Sleek, can lights low
I try very blatantly
with my dingy date
story to show off
how, on this couch,
I am the funniest
He tries to give me
the cold shoulder,
and his is very bony
I grasp its pale, damp
circumference, and it's
like holding whitefish
Then he gives me his
hand, which is softer
than any girl's—lax
feeling, balmy, and on it,
I scribble things in italics,
in a winding language
that he doesn't know,
and he shouts in what
he thinks is contralto
for a translator, but

his voice is translucent,
and the other natives
don't ever hear him
We laugh somehow,
and I see his eyes
in brisk flashes like
ever-present parts of
whatever's happening,
and I think about how
he's about to move places
and take this very house
that we're now drunk in
as his own and maybe
the forced community
will somehow warm
something inside him
In-joke I say that he hates
me and ask him to be kinder
and he gives me, kindly,
a frosty 350, and I know
that it has a cooling
cullet shell but that
it warms the soul—as he thirstily puts it,
and his eyes are too
bright like chemicals
Neck the shoulder
Neck it neck it neck it
The gifted shoulder
Too cold and hot,
and like a new home
with OK roommates

Who in the living fuck
even calls it necking
anymore, are you
eighty years young?
Cool flashes, warmth
shouldering me into
a cold stupor . . .

Coma Black

Matthew McCain

Hooksett, New Hampshire - United States

Your coma black conscience is ready
Like so many times before, it's time to demure the hopes with sedation
Another needle goes in to satisfy the fixation
If you're not seeing the end, it's probably the medication

Hopeless cadavers are spread across the basement
Some of them you know by name
A taunting addiction that just won't let go
It's just another game that'll determine your fate

When the high can't get any higher, when the low can't get any lower
When you're paralyzed on your back and there's no way of getting back
All you are is another coma black

Doctors come and go and swirl all around
To get a good look at another botched experiment
Now it's just another void of torture and torment
As you lay on the slab of metal unaware and dormant

And now you're just another lonely cadaver
That never even mattered
You tried to be idealistic
But ended up being only a statistic

When the high can't get any higher, when the low can't get any lower
When you're down and out and can't find your way back
You'll realize what it's like to live in coma black

Finders Keepers

Keirdan Haslam

Burgaw, North Carolina - United States

In shadows deep, where secrets creep,
A chilling game, a twisted leap.
A treasure sought, a prize unknown,
A whispered tale, a haunting tone.

"Finders keepers," so they say,
A twisted rule, a cruel display.
A stolen heart, a shattered mind,
A darkness left, a void to find.

With eyes ablaze and hearts aflame,
They search for riches, lost to shame.
But in the shadows, where the truth resides,
A chilling secret, deep inside.

For in the darkness, where the shadows creep,
A haunting whisper, a chilling leap.
"Finders keepers," so they say,
A twisted rule, a cruel display.

Finders Keepers

Âmi Jey

Mammoth Cave, Kentucky - United States

I found it by accident, a forgotten treasure—
a shard of light wedged in the crease of a long-abandoned drawer.
"Finders keepers," I whispered, alone,
while the world spun, heedless, indifferent,
unaware of the moment lost in the shadows.
It wasn't gold or silver,
not a diamond or a ring,
but something more delicate, more dangerous—
a fragment of memory, a ghost of a forgotten song
that stung when I let it surface.
"Finders keepers," I murmur again,
but the words fall flat,
empty in my mouth,
because what's found is always fractured,
never the whole, just a piece of the past.
Still, I clutch it close—
as if it might whisper the secrets I'm afraid to know—
about love, about loss, about the ache that never lets go.
"Finders keepers," I say once more,
for in finding it,
I've begun to stitch together the torn seams
of who I thought I lost forever.

Finders Keepers

Johannes Berriman

Sint-Gillis-Waas - Belgium

Finders keepers
On my days off, I dive into work,
Grinding at dreams that don't pay,
Wondering if this is living,
Or just a way to fill the time.

Finding Flames

Cole Allison

Maple Grove, Minnesota - United States

Seems cliché,
but with the right people it is more than that.
Water turns to rock,
what seemed uninhabitable,
is now a frozen desert.
The snow crunches,
wind whips,
stars dance,
and coyotes cry.
Matches are the only thing that will,
light a flame,
create a memory,
start a conversation.
Warm flames imitate the sun,
where there is none.
The flames thaw the ice,
that freezes your heart.
And the smoke disintegrates

worries,
burdens,
secrets.
Fire on ice.
Is more than just crimson flames,
it's a rebel flame in the never-ending darkness,
a spark of hope under the frozen sky.

B'TWIN

Finding Yourself

Akshay Sonthalia

Mumbai - India

This voyage faced many roadblocks;
Led to realizing, what it felt like —
to get lost . . .

Oh! Those jitters brought by unsettled moments, and;
Silently brewing anxiety tolls, and;
This trailing strained hope that never ceased and believed that —

This is the way forward,
eventually finding thyself,
As being the true purpose behind it all.

When, the world is one's homeground.
There's no question about -
getting lost.

Yet, the voyage does begin with that feeling for real:
which today I realize was an illusion, —
As if you're losing yourself, you're lost.

Guilt In The Rain

Irin Chung

Saipan - Northern Mariana Islands

Left my umbrella, where has it gone?
Once it was mine, but now it's moved on.
Someone left theirs, who has lost?
Eyes glued to it, at what cost?
Rain keeps falling, I need a shield.
Someone left theirs, I need to be healed.

Whispered quietly, "Finders keepers,"
Endless guilt drips with the rain.
Endless doubt spins through my brain.
Pitter-patter pitter-patter,
Eager hands reach, but is this right?
Really hoping someone finds my shield.
So I can feel this guilt concealed.

I'm So Lucky

Mark Tochen

Camas, Washington - United States

a love story as a prose poem

I found an old picture my wife-to-be coming through the
graduation line at college a wonderful student a wonderful
companion her school friends loved to invite her home for the
holidays and their parents instantly fell in love with her
as did I but I am the one who got to keep her by my side for a
lifetime *finders keepers* says the old schoolyard claim

in school she won many honors and her graduation picture
was perfect a demure beautiful young woman with a little smile
on her face and wise young eyes calmly proclaiming I've got this
I'm ready she was poised she was lovely she was the full essence
of herself even in her early twenties
and I could only smile when I found the old graduation picture
and looked on her image with great joy and great satisfaction
murmuring to myself the schoolboy phrase for claiming a
treasure *finders keepers*

and where was I as she embarked on more education and then
began a career I was still in school commuting to my summer
job on a tiny Japanese motorcycle to a twelve-hour night shift

in a hot and steamy factory manufacturing fishing supplies for commercial fishermen and at three am I would go to the all-night laundromat next to the factory and get a cold Coke from the vending machine and walking outside look up at the starry sky and with a little smile thought of her my lady far away but I was certain she would be my lady I knew because after all *finders keepers*

years after her graduation picture we met and courted and married sharing the future as one I survived the draft we moved across the country as a couple and have two lovely kids now lovely adults and now in our sixth decade of marriage in my advanced years I still take delight in the schoolboy claim *finders keepers*

It's A Rarity, So

Carissa Cardenas

Eustis, Florida - United States

Friend found in a wine lounge—
I don't frequent these kinds of places.
Novel sisterhood, birthed where it did not thrive;
Determined silently, we'd both rather be home reading,
Each feeling restless in the mutual misplacement of the night,
Ready to rush home for fresh citrus tea and book roulette, though
Steinfield and Cather have hardly waited up for people like you
and me.

Keeping our friendship steady through life's waken
metamorphosis—
Embroidery, flowerpot painting, and sourdough baking.
Elevating our dearly beloveds with brick-built words,
Pleasant talk-walks through the produce market,
Eating the other's fresh homecooked meals.
Ribbon-haired friend, dear golden thread
Solidly woven into my life, here to stay.

finders keepers.

Journey

Shulin Ho

Hong Kong

When mother arrived home five past seven at the dawn of sunset
during the time when the beams of light gradually levied their
force, we were already done with Play Time,
and were ready for Dinner.
Of course, I embraced her with open arms (like usual),
similarly to how I would hug Ba Ba. Perhaps, I might've thought
of mother like
Ba Ba, but I don't think she really is that much of an importance
to me considering how she never spends time with me and how
much longer her absence feels to me.

No words come out of her mouth,
in the time that it takes to sit down.
Tables
and
tables
of the Food we would eat but mother said we could have a
Special Dinner today because she was 'in a good mood' or
something.

I don't quite Remember what she said.

Sushi, Cucumber, Char Siu and a fusion of what auntie would cook only on Special Occasions.
Using my left hand, I tried to pick a jumbo piece of Char Siu with my newly learnt Fai Zi skills (chopsticks technique) while Journey scrambled to find his Fai Zi to take a piece.

'Finders Keepers!' I yelled at him,
with a flashing smile across my face.
Journey screamed back at me but
I don't really remember what he said but it was something along the lines
of how Finders Keepers doesn't apply to Food but I just remember smiling
like a Star in the quiet night sky and not caring much because
Ba Ba said food was first-come-first-served.

'It's mine!' I remember Journey exclaiming, his eyes blinking with anger.

Ba Ba told him to calm down but he just couldn't.

Tender tears forcefully paved their path through his cheekbones as he held out his hands in protest like branches on a solemn winter night. His eyes glistened with desolated annoyance that swam through his veins down to his heart and back to his eyes and back down to his heart. It was like – I don't know – he just couldn't control himself. He just . . . he just – couldn't control himself. Or that's what I thought to myself, but I knew something that I didn't know.

Watching him open his mouth, I expected to hear words dive out. Instead of the raving, tempered speech I expected, I was met with a booming silence trickling down the corner of his mouth. As his hands convulsed in the hushed anger of his unsatisfied frustration, my heart started beating louder: da dum, da dum, da dum. Like how my drum teacher taught me in school, da dum, da dum, da dum.

How my feelings seemed to underpin and undermine my thoughts, I don't know, but during that stressfully bitter sound of my brother's tears levitating down to his blue 'UConn' sweatshirt, my heart started slowing down – quieter: da dum, da dum, da dum. As I think about the pain and frustration in his eyes, I see myself, da dum, da dum, da dum. I think I felt bad for him.

The pain of my brother reverberating at me, sparking a war in every nerve cell in my body, the pain of my silence, staring back at my reflection on the glass table. Da dum, da dum, da dum.

Now, I'm 17, and perhaps, I did love Journey. Perhaps through the fights and arguments and the timeouts that we spent with each other staring at Ba Ba's posters that were stuck on his wall, perhaps I did love Journey. No, I do, I love him.

I love my brother.

Da dum.

Losing, And Finding

Roselyne Omondi

Nairobi - Kenya

Can I offer you anything today, *chale*?
Tomorrow, my friend
Today, I was just passing by; should I have said so?
Tomorrow, I'll not drop in on you, like a thief
Today, no time to tell you what I found
Tomorrow, I'll bring some things to cook
Today, your kitchen looks empty, you see
Tomorrow, I'll tell Jolly not to roast on wood fire
Today, I'm not *really* hungry
Tomorrow, I'll come with a turning, groaning, gurgling tummy
Today, I don't want to bother you
Tomorrow, I'll have banana or orange, no prep
I'll have cheesecake, no bake
I'll take shortcut tea and boiling *chai* with milk
I'll let you use your white cast iron pots and smeg burner for me
I'll let you make sea fish and salad on a bed of squash with butter
Tomorrow will not come, *chale*
Tonight, I leave for another land, my friend; should I have told you?
I leave, with my finder – he will keep me
Like finders keepers.

Minesweeper

Ian Seppala

Oakfield, New York - United States

Minesweeper
Unlucky life of minesweepers
Seeking pain for good purpose
Common refrain of finders keepers
Seems awfully perverse

LOST CAT

More Than Just A Doll

Chris Loy

San Marcos, Texas - United States

You set your doll down and walked away, fascinated by a newer shinier doll that wasn't as safe.
The new doll was thrilling and made you come to life.
Your old reliable just sat by alone waiting for you to come back.
Days turned into weeks turned into months and all you ever showed was scorn.
Scorn for the love, scorn for the support, scorn for the readiness to keep being there for you.
Time and again you would come back and tease, never committing, knowing your doll wouldn't go anywhere.
One time when you were off playing though, I found your doll all alone.
Sparking eyes were hurting yet beautiful, body and soul crushed yet still amazing.
I picked your doll up from the corner where you left it and never set it down again.
Finders keepers.
You still don't understand the treasure you lost but I will hold it forever.

He was too good for you.

One Summer Evening At Donaghmore Church And Round Tower

Gavin Bourke

Navan - Ireland

The graveyard trees stood higher than the ruins of the church
and the perfectly intact round tower of bricks and mortar.
We entered the open site through the unlocked gates
and walked the narrow path up the hill among the gravestones.
Saint Patrick was here before us founding a monastery
in the 5th century, the tower built between the 11th and 12th
centuries
a truly colossal and spectacular local presence
the remains of the 16th-century church encouraging the mind's
eye
to complete the full picture.

Surrounded by headstones, some dating back hundreds of years
the epitaphs barely legible in some cases, others of blank stone
worn to discolouration by the unforgiving elements over time.

The open windows of the tower facing the light in all directions
high crosses surrounded by ornate metal frames
nameless iron crosses scattered throughout the cemetery.

A stone bench by the wall in memory of an unnamed person
hard not to be touched by the commemoration.
Walking through history by the graves of those who have passed recently
sharing the soil with those who died hundreds of years before them.
The sun came out unexpectedly illuminating the grass and the daisies
improving the legibility of the headstones, some of fresh inscriptions
etched in new stone and polished marble.

The sunlight shone through the trees like stained glass windows
that lit up the whole sacred site with a bright light
almost as if painting the picture with a kind of reverence
a natural quietness to the scene as if intended by the founders
peaceful, serene and steeped deep in reverence.

Penny For Your Thoughts?

Addie Hemsley

Burley, Idaho - United States

I love pennies.
I always have
and suppose I always will.
They're unique,
so different from their
brothers and sisters;
dimes and quarters and nickels.
Metallic copper with smooth sides.
I don't care about nickel or zinc,
nor their sparkling silver faces.

In the eyes of society,
they are worth next to nothing,
and yet they are here.
They are something.
Most people spot the little piece of treasure
and continue on their way.
Even worse they throw them out,
denounce their worth because,
"It's just a penny"
and never give a second thought.

I think about those people often.
Good luck, as the saying goes,
isn't the only thing they are missing.

I imagine the hands that have
touched his surface;
weathered and cracked from hard work,
now buying dinner for his family.
Busy with the insanity called life,
tossing the small coin in the tips cup.

I collect them in a glass-blown
jar with a piece of cork
sealing them in place.
I could take the time to count each coin–
note its birthdate and where it came to be.
The condition of its skin–
newborns in a dying world,
others mint from oxidation.
But I don't.
I love them just the way they are.

THIS NOTE IS LEGAL TENDER
FOR ALL DEBTS, PUBLIC AND
Treasurer of the United States

Pushed Underwater, Confront The Monsters

Whitney Leshay P.

South Bend, Indiana - United States

In inky depths, I stand paralyzed,
A statue carved from fear and doubt.
Before me, void; behind, the known—
Both paths obscured by murky shroud.

Days bleed to nights, time loses form,
As I reach blindly for a guide.
But hands grasp only empty space,
And hope, like air, is long denied.

The pressure builds, a liquid vice,
Crushing lungs and clouding mind.
Entwined in tendrils of the deep,
I thrash against the ties that bind.

Spectral forms drift through the gloom,
Echoes of a brighter past.
I claw through layers of my dread,
Each movement slow, each breath my last.

The current's song, a siren's call,
Beckons me to cease my fight.
But something stirs within my core,
A spark, defiant in the night.

With bloodied hands and battered soul,
I scale the mountain of my fears.
Each scar a map, each bruise a star,
Guiding me through unseen years.

At last, I breach the surface tension,
Gasping as I taste the light.
The sun, a long-forgotten friend,
Embraces me with warmth so bright.
I shed the weight of watery tombs,
And demons lose their fearsome might.
For I have walked through darkest depths,
And emerged, unbroken, into sight.

No more shall I peer back below,
Where shadows lurk and monsters dwell.
My spirit, forged in lightless realms,
Now rings with freedom's clearest bell.

Second Thoughts

Cole Allison

Maple Grove, Minnesota - United States

The man on the moon stares,
right back at us.
Clutch goes in,
and exhaust fumes pour.
Headlights fight the darkness,
the swirling snow grabs your remaining heat,
as the RPMs run through your body.
Nothing but snowy ground,
three idiots,
looming lumps of ice,
and worries that are only 10 feet in front of you.
The trees are a blur,
trail gets skinnier,
40 feels more like 60.
Emerged in it now
no backing out.
Locked in by the trees
and speed locked by the ice.
Scared of,
sliding,
crashing,
flipping,
but it is a boy's trip.

The Back Corner

Alyssa Kathleen

Stuart, Florida - United States

In the back corner of the room—just there.

Can you see it?
The shreds of my dignity, left behind—woven words of affirmations that I tell myself to soothe wounds that are still healing. *I deserve better. I deserve love. I know what I'm worth.*
You know—bullshit like that.
These words sit on my tongue, heavy and stale, falling flat like the ginger ale we kept too long in the fridge. The same ginger ale I drank when I was nauseous—*always so nauseous.* I never considered that the whirling in my stomach wasn't sickness. It was the chaos of loving you.
Maybe that's all I'm good for—being recycled. Spun around, worn thin by a chaotic empty kind of love. Just another can left on the counter with a dent in it. Just another naive phrase stuck to the wall, starting to peel away. Nothing new, nothing important. Only the pieces of me that aren't sticky anymore, left behind.
I guess that's how it works, right?

Some of us just settle for the leftovers.

Finders keepers.

So take the rest of me—take what you've already stolen. It's okay if you leave me the ugly, sticky, broken parts. I can handle the self-hatred, the embarrassment of giving you a thousand chances and never giving myself one.
So do you see it?
Right there.
In the back corner of the room.
The part of me still holding onto all this pain for you.

The Blue

Jana Tvorogova

Paris - France

Suddenly, he woke up on a road and could not remember anything
He did not see the road at first
The first thing he saw was the blue sky above him
It seemed just as endless as the road

Since the road seemed so infinite
he had no choice but to get up and walk
Maybe he could shorten the road by doing so

While he was walking, he noticed some flowers, bluebells
A poem immediately popped into his head
"Find keepers!" he said. *"It's my poem."*

I must have been a great poet, he figured
since for everything he has seen, a fitting poem just popped into his head
He walked the road accompanied by poetry
describing the surroundings with beautiful poems

I wonder if poets also have blue periods, he thought
as he gazed towards the sky

He continued his lonesome walk
One week later, after he had arrived in a town
and had been helped to find his way home
he made a discovery

Nothing seemed familiar to him at home
but they assured him that this was indeed his house
He wandered from room to room with no purpose
almost wishing himself back on the long road

He came across a bookshelf
By flipping through the books
he read all the poems that had popped into his mind that day on the road
He had written none of the poems himself

The Diamond Ring

Aayaz Ali Khan

Delhi - India

That diamond ring,
As large as a fancy cufflink,
Shined like stars with moon's cold,
Embellished upon the sun,
Envied and desired by all of Eve's daughters,
Yet it went to her daughter-in-law.

Dragged by hair into that capacious hall,
All saw the sparkle on those swollen hands.
Each gaze coveted it, for their mistress of passion or law,
But that was to be settled later.

Curves and edges, all stripped bare,
Drillings done, each man in his turn.
So did I, unable to find release,
After all, it's the fifth,
Oh, that I am shy.

Then the whole was divided into parts,
The only part worthy of interest:
The symmetrical bone adorned with thin flesh, milky skin, and long nail.

Once the embellishment was gone, no one cared,
All equally scorched, no part spared.

Everyone screamed finders keepers,
But, to everyone's dismay,
The leader of the faceless demanded the flake of snow,
And so, it embellished new hands to make new stories and carry the old.

The Road

Cole Allison

Maple Grove, Minnesota - United States

Never in a rush,
always grabbing candy at the gas station.
Heated seats and warm air in the winter,
and windows wide with shirts off in the summer.
Music is always blasting but not too loud to where you can't hear
Ben in the back.
Speeding,
watching,
hearing,
calmness is out the window,
every word builds the excitement,
finding its way to my heart.
No restrictions other than,
be home by 8am on Sunday.
Finding a place to eat is the only concern.
Don't care where you are going,
or how to get there,
boy's trip.

The Joy Of Being Alive

Aviva Derenowski

Staten Island, New York - United States

i'm a jew who asks what's a jew i'm a woman who asks what's
a woman i'm a person who asks what's a person and why am i
asking because there are jews who are nothing like me women
who are alien to me and people who are my complete opposite
so how come we are one how come so many of us are related
because we want to love and belong and not as finders keepers
we want to be part of something immense and transparent huge
and meaningful like the sky and the ocean and all beings in
between i'm a part and so are you we are not identical we are not
harmonious but we want to fit in and forgive all our oppressors
real and imagined forgiveness will set us free from guilt,
resentment and vengeance it's the first step to being a sensible
person part of a sensible community that extends compassion
to those we don't understand we pray and hope one day we
will understanding them will open the opportunity for them to
understand us that will be the day when heaven and earth are
one and nobody will stay behind because there is no behind it's
all one front of magic and sensibility love acceptance friendship
and heartfelt hugs and cuddles like puppies in a global puppy pile
feeling the joy of being alive together

Time Travel At My Day Job

Basil Wilcox

Ypsilanti, Michigan - United States

I know the woods aren't very thick here, but we grew up in the woods, you and me, little wolves with all the practice of making trees what we want. I am at my work desk now googling *"what makes sunsets pink?"* making these double monitors what I want. Light scatters thin enough for pink to reach us and the little wolf in me blows you a kiss. Finders keepers. What I want: the atmosphere carrying its wavelengths to you. And it is our only one. Atmosphere, I mean. Scattering back to you and me, yesterday stomping in our big, big woods outside the window. And you, ten and gathering supplies for the apocalypse. In another woods, the kiss I just blew tells a smaller you *"yes, pick that one!"* and when you find the stick, when its soil sticks to your palm, when you ask the atmosphere *"is this the one? the stick that will protect our home?"* there it lands on your cheek to scatter its light to you with *yes, yes, yes this will protect your home. Your home will be protected, wolf.*

Upon Finding You

Âmi Jey

Mammoth Cave, Kentucky - United States

I found you like a jagged stone
hidden in the cracks of life's unspoken places,
a treasure forgotten by the world,
waiting for me to see the weight of it.
"Finders keepers," I murmur,
but the words feel too small, too shallow—
for I've found more than just a lover,
I've found the mirror to my soul,
the fire that burns the edges of my own desolation.
You are not just a moment in time,
but a universe colliding with mine,
a raw tenderness carved from the rubble
of everything I've survived.
"Finders keepers," I say again,
but it's not a claim—it's a declaration,
a vow to never release what I've come to know
as the pulse of my own heart.
I will love you until the world fades,
until there is nothing left to give but all of me,
until your name is the only sound in my blood.

NOT
FOR HIRE

What's Left

Johannes Berriman

Sint-Gillis-Waas - Belgium

Maybe we would've made it,
in some other version of this mess.
You, always pulling away,
but somehow, I still feel you too close,
like smoke on my clothes after a night out—
something I can't lose.

What I find doesn't match the words;
they've changed shape,
like how shadows do at dusk.

Endings? Who even knows what those are.
They never look like what you want.
But there's a comfort in knowing you've lost,
in knowing it's over.
And still, somehow, somehow, we're still here—
finders keepers, or what's left of it.

When Stars Start To Cry

Sailee Charlu

Newport Beach, California - United States

I wonder if his memory loss started at the top or bottom, like meteors flung into the sky, their edges too sharp to hold. I watched his life like a sheet of rain, flickering until it became a canvas of ache. Nostalgia stretching out, shapeless and endless, a tide pulling at things I didn't know could break. Suppose the stars are just our grief reflected back on us. Proof that sorrow has no home but everywhere. I realized there's no use in scrolling over photos, zooming to every story whispering from his skin. I watched him vanish, bit by bit, into the space he left behind, until he couldn't zoom out anymore. A signalless satellite. Until the zooming, and the scrolling, and the weight of my love folds inward. Until my picture of him shifts and crackles, becoming a pixelated image. Where I don't know if my mind is my mind, or a creation of my own synapses. Just as starlings strive without rest, their fractured wings like windpipes, broken but still fighting. Our minds tangle in the gray of it all, his absence bleeding into me. Euphoric and sharp. Where I can't tell where I stop and he starts. There are moments, he showed me that love is the ache that lingers, ringing out of the center of a guitar collected like wilted stems at the bottom of a vase. It's the unquenchable desire to reach across silence even when it swallows you whole. It's a body with a bleeding orphan inside. It's a dance done on burning

GRATIS
Bananas

kites while dreaming at the speed of light. It's a light that surfaces in the shipwreck of your sleep. And so I wear my grandpa's memories for him, like a tiny god on my sleeve, bringing me closer to something greater. I want to think that everything happens for a reason but the stars only offer silence—scattered, nameless, and burning in the dark.

You Are Found

Ryan Gourley

Cochrane, Alberta - Canada

confusion shouldn't be in my head right now,
it makes perfect sense, anyone would say so.

the throbbing behind my eyes built
as i realized, truly realized, that you
were no longer holding onto
the string we had strung.

the tears never came, the headache from
holding them back caused more pain
than i could have thought.

it was a sobering realization,
someone had found you.

i felt like a useless child,
being told finders keepers
after losing sight of a rolling coin.

i had searched for you,
you had searched for me,

there were fleeting moments,
moments where we caught wind,
noticed each other's scent.

when storms rolled in,
i could hear your screams
through the buffeting winds,
reminding me you were so, so close.

but we never found each other.

Waiting

Roselyne

Nairobi - Kenya

You were to be here, at Shore's
Whooshing, swishing, burping
Bringing forth suds; cleansing
A whale of ocean's prickies; delivering
Prickies that poke the heel like a syringe
Here, caressing earth's grit
Grit that is like sandpaper
Bringing finds, for a finder's keeper
You are there, with Horizon
Your break, after dragging in last night's catch
Without basket or net
Without boat or trawler
I long for you, for your return to Shore's
To swish between my toes
To marinate my leggings in brine
To put my midnight thoughts to rest
With your swish! swash! whoosh!
Crashing on the rocks
Beneath coconut trees.

Acknowledgement

Irin Chung

Mark Tochen

Mark Tochen is Previously Published In

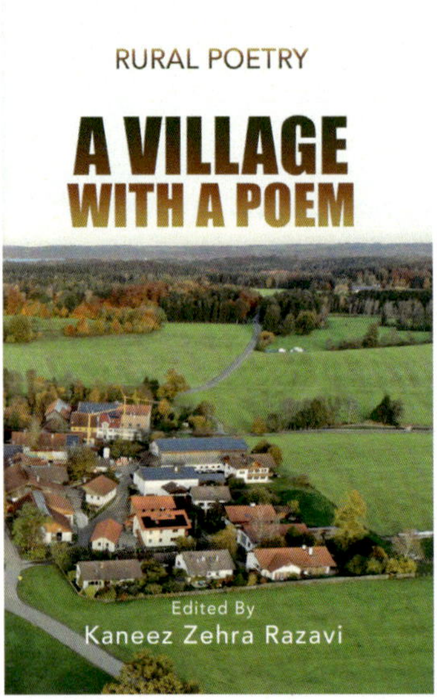

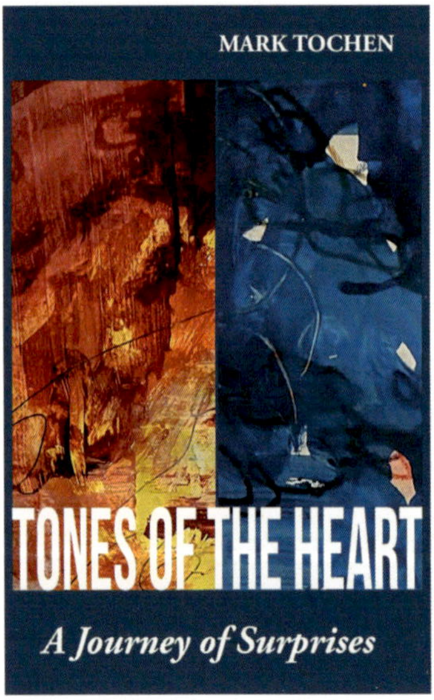